HALLOWEEN JOKES FOR KIDS

FUNNY ZOMBIE JOKES
FOR CHILDREN

1

1. **What do ghosts enjoy eating for supper?**

    Answer: Spooketi

~~~~~~~~~~~~~~~~~~~~~~~

2. **What do you do when 50 zombies surround your house?**

    Answer: Well, you hope its Halloween.

3. Where do ghosts typically buy their food?

Answer: At a ghost-ry store.

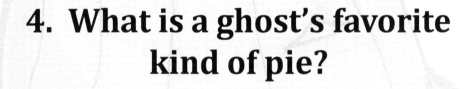

4. What is a ghost's favorite kind of pie?

Answer: Booberry pie

5. What do you get when you cross a vampire with a loud duck?

Answer: Count Quakula.

~~~~~~~~~~

6. What do vampires take when they get sick?

Answer: Coffin drops.

7. What did one ghost say to the other?

Answer: Do you believe in humans?

~~~~~~~~~~~~

8. What goes around a haunted house but never ever stops?

Answer: A fence.

9. Why are skeletons so rude?

Answer: They don't have a heart.

~~~~~~~~~~

10. What did one owl say to another owl?

Answer: Happy Owl-oween.

11. Why do ghost make such good cheerleaders?

Answer: They have a ton of spirit.

~~~~~~~~

12. What kind of pants do ghosts wear when trick or treating?

Answer: Boo jeans.

13. What do you get when you cross a snowman with a vampire?

Answer: Frostbite.

~~~~~~~~

14. What does a witch use to keep her hair nice?

Answer: Scare spray.

15. What did the skeleton say before dinner time?

Answer: Bone appetite.

~~~~~~~~

16. What is a ghost's favorite kind of fruit?

Answer: Boo berries.

17. What do many mom's dress up as on Halloween?

Answer: Mummies.

~~~~~~~~~~~~~~~

18. What do you get when you cross a Cocker Spaniel, a ghost, and a poodle?

Answer: A cocker poodle boo

19. What do birds say on Halloween?

Answer: Twig or tweet.

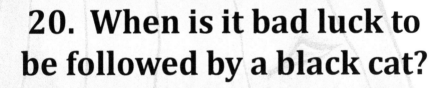

20. When is it bad luck to be followed by a black cat?

Answer: When you are a mouse.

21. What kind of dessert do ghosts like?

Answer: I scream.

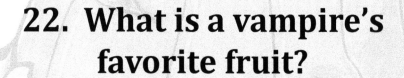

22. What is a vampire's favorite fruit?

Answer: Neck tarine.

23. What do you get when you cross a witch with sand?

Answer: A sandwich.

24. What do ghosts use to wash their hair?

Answer: Shamboo.

25. Why is Superman's costume so tight?

Answer: Because he wears a size S.

~~~~~~~~~~~~

26. Who did Frankenstein take to thedance?

Answer: His ghoul friend.

27. Why are ghosts so bad at lying?

Answer: Because you can always see right through them.

~~~~~~~

28. What room do ghosts not need?

Answer: A living room.

29. What do you call a pumpkin that is fat?

Answer: A plumpkin.

~~~~~~~~~~

30. What did the little girl say when she had to choose between a bike and candy?

Answer: Trike or treat.

31. Why did the skeleton go to the movies alone?

Answer: He had no body to go with.

~~~~~~~~~~

32. Why did the skeleton cross the road?

Answer: To get to the body shop.

33. Why did the skeleton refuse to cross the road?

Answer: He didn't have the guts.

~~~~~~~~~~~

34. Why did the skeleton not go to school?

Answer: His heart wasn't in it.

35. What is the most important subject that a witch will learn in school?

Answer: Spelling.

~~~~~~~~~~

36. What did Dracula say after hearing a joke?

Answer: That joke sucked.

37. Where do vampires keep their most of their money?

Answer: The blood bank.

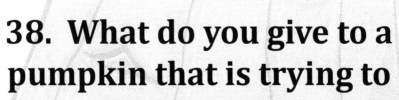

38. What do you give to a pumpkin that is trying to quit smoking?

Answer: A pumpkin patch.

39. Why do cemeteries have fences around them?

Answer: Because people are dying to get in.

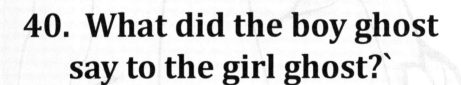

40. What did the boy ghost say to the girl ghost?`

Answer: You are so bootiful.

41. What was the mummies' vacation like?

Answer: Hard to say; they were too wrapped up.

~~~~~~~~~

42. What is in a ghost's nose?

`

Answer: Boogers.

43. What is a ghost's favorite food?

Answer: Hamboogers.

~~~~~~~~~~~~~~~~

44. What is Dracula's favorite restaurant?

Answer: Murder King.

45. What did Dracula have for dessert?

Answer: Whine and ice scream.

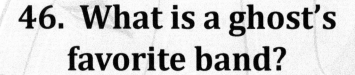

46. What is a ghost's favorite band?

Answer: The Boo's Brothers.

47. What did the goblin say to the witch?

Answer: I don't know, why don't you tell me?

48. How did the ghost say goodbye to the vampire?

Answer: So long, sucker.

49. Why can't skeletons lift weights?

Answer: They are all bones and no muscle.

~~~~~~~~~~~~~~~~

50. Why do ghost ride elevators?

Answer: It lifts their spirits.

51. What is a witch in the desert called?

Answer: A sandwich.

~~~~~~~~~~

52. What did the teenage witch ask her mom witch on Halloween?

Answer: Can I have the keys to the broom tonight?

53. Where do ghosts go for fun?

Answer: The boo-vies.

~~~~~~~~~~~~~~~~

54. What is a ghost's favorite type of car?

Answer: A boo-ik.

55. What is a skeleton's favorite song?

Answer: Bad to the Bone

~~~~~~~~~~

56. What is a vampire's least favorite song?

Answer: Another One Bites the Dust.

57. Why do skeleton's drink milk?

Answer: To give them strong bones.

～～～～～～

58. What do you call a monster who poisons corn flakes?

Answer: A cereal killer.

59. Why don't ghosts have bands?

Answer: They would get booed.

~~~~~~~~~~~~~~~~

60. Why did the vampire need mouthwash?

Answer: He had bat breath.

61. Why was the mummy so tense?

Answer: He was wound too tight.

~~~~~~~~~~~~~~

62. What did the corpse mom do when her son was bad?

Answer: Ground him.

63. What did the mother ghost say to her children ghost in the car?

Answer: Fasten your sheet belts.

64. Why did the man with the knife in his head cross the road?

Answer: He was just dying to get to the other side.

65. Why don't mummies go on vacation?

Answer: They are afraid to unwind.

〰〰〰〰〰

66. What do you call two witches living together?

Answer: Broom mates.

67. What do you call a witches garage?

Answer: A broom closet.

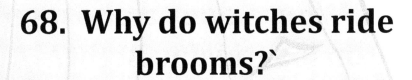

68. Why do witches ride brooms?`

Answer: Vacuum cleaners get stuck at the end of the cord.

69. Where do ghosts go to get their hair done?

Answer: A boo-ty shop.

~~~~~~~~~

70. Where does a ghost go on a Saturday night?

Answer: Anywhere he can boogie

71. Where does a ghost go on a vacation?

Answer: Mali-boo.

~~~~~~~~~~~

72. What do ghosts drink at breakfast?

Answer: Coffee with scream and sugar.

73. When does a ghost have breakfast?

Answer: In the moaning.

~~~~~~~~~~

74. What type of dog does a vampire have?

Answer: A bloodhound.

75. What kind of tie does a ghost wear?

Answer: A boo-tie.

~~~~~~~~~

76. What is a ghost's favorite sale?

Answer: A white sale.

77. Why did the headless horseman go into sales?

Answer: He wanted to get a head in life.

~~~~~~~~~~

78. What can't you give the headless horseman?

Answer: A headache.

79. How do you keep a monster from biting his nails?

Answer: You give him screws.

~~~~~~~~~~~~~~~~

80. Why did Dracula take cough syrup?

Answer: To stop his coffin.

81. What kind of gum does a ghost chew?

Answer: Boo Boo gum.

~~~~~~~~~

82. What kind of key does a skeleton use?

Answer: A skeleton key.

83. Who does Dracula get letters from?

Answer: His fang club.

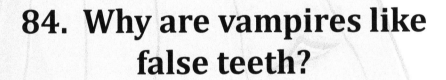

84. Why are vampires like false teeth?

Answer: They all come out at night.

85. Why did Dracula go to the dentist?

Answer: He had a terrible fang ache.

~~~~~~~~~

86. Why does everyone hate Dracula?

Answer: He has a bat temper.

87. What is it called when a vampire has trouble with his house?

Answer: A grave problem.

~~~~~~~~~~

88. What is a vampire's least favorite food?

Answer: Steak.

89. How do vampires flirt?

Answer: They bat their eyes.

~~~~~~~~~~

90. What did the mummy movie director say at the end of the scene?

Answer: Okay, that's a wrap.

91. What is Dracula's least favorite song?

Answer: Sunshine on my Shoulders.

~~~~~~~~

92. How do you know when a vampire has been at a donut shop?

Answer: All the jelly is sucked out of the jelly donuts.

93. What is it like to be kissed by a vampire?

Answer: It's a pain in the neck.

~~~~~~~~~~

94. How do you know that vampire's like baseball?

Answer: Each night they turn into a bat.

95. Why do vampire's scare people?

Answer: They are bored to death.

~~~~~~~~~

96. What is a vampire's favorite place on the net?

Answer: www. Halloween .com

97. What instrument do skeleton's play?

Answer: Trombone.

~~~~~~~~~~

98. Why do ghosts shiver and moan?

Answer: It's cold and drafty under there.

99. What do you get when you cross a squash with a pumpkin?

Answer: A squashed pumpkin pie.

~~~~~~~~~~~~~~~

100. What do you get when you cross a black cat with a lemon?

Answer: A sour pus.

101. What do monsters call their parents?

Answer: Mummy and Daddy.

~~~~~~~~~~~~~~~~~~~~

102. Why did the skeleton go disco dancing?

Answer: To see the boogie man.

103. What do Italian's eat on Halloween?

Answer: Fettuccini Afraido.

~~~~~~~~~~

104. Where does a ghost refuel his car?

Answer: At a ghast station.

105. Where do goblins live?

Answer: In North and South Scarolina.

~~~~~~~~~~~~~~~~

106. Where do werewolves live?

Answer: In Howlywood, California.

107. What did Dracula visit in New York?

Answer: The Vampire State Building.

~~~~~~~~~~

108. What is the most famous French skeleton?

Answer: Napoleon Bone Apart.

109. What was the most famous skeleton detective?

Answer: Sherlock Bones.

~~~~~~~~

110. What do you call two spiders that just got hitched?

Answer: Newlywebs.

111. What was the most famous ghost detective of all-time?

Answer: Sherlock Moans.

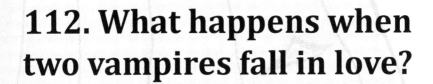

112. What happens when two vampires fall in love?

Answer: It is love at first bite.

113. What kind of makeup do ghosts wear?

Answer: Mas-Scare-A.

~~~~~~~~~~

114. What is a vampire's favorite holiday?

Answer: Fangsgiving.

115. What are a ghost's favorite kind of streets?

Answer: Dead ends.

~~~~~~~~~~~~

116. What do you give a skeleton on Valentine's Day?

Answer: Bones in a heart shaped box.

117. What do you put on a ghosts ice cream sundae?

Answer: Whipped scream.

~~~~~~~~~~

118. Why did the vampire read the Wall Street Journal?

Answer: He heard it had good circulation.

119. What do you call a ghost who gets too close to a fire?

Answer: A toasty ghosty.

~~~~~~~~~

120. Why are ghost's messy eaters?

Answer: They are always goblin.

121. Why did Dracula let the doctor look at his throat?`

Answer: He had been coffin.

~~~~~~~~~~

122. Where did the goblin throw the football?

Answer: Over the ghoul line.

123. What happens when a ghosts is lost in fog?

Answer: He is mist.

24. Where does Dracula eat his lunch?

Answer: At the casketeria.

125. Why did the game warden arrest the ghost?

Answer: He didn't have a haunting license.

~~~~~~~~~~~~~~~~

126. Why was the girl afraid of the vampire?

Answer: He was all bite and no bark.

127. Why do ghosts go to bars?

Answer: For the boos.

~~~~~~~~~

128. What do ghosts say when something is really neat?

Answer: Ghoul.

129. What did the skeleton say to the vampire?

Answer: You suck.

~~~~~~

130. What is a monster's favorite bean?

Answer: A human bean.

131. Why do demon's and ghoul's hang out together?

Answer: Because a demon is a ghoul's best friend.

~~~~~~~~

132. What is a mummy's favorite type of music?

Answer: Wrap.

133. What do ghost's drink on Halloween?

Answer: Ghoul-Aid.

~~~~~~~~~~~~~~~~~~~~~~~

134. What do eye doctors give out on Halloween?

Answer: Candy corneas.

135. What do you call wood when it's scared?

Answer: Petrified.

~~~~~~~~~~~~~~~~

136. What is a ghost's favorite ride at the fair?

Answer: The Scary-Go-Round.

137. What's worse than being a 5 ton witch?

Answer: Being her broom.

~~~~~~~~~~~~~

138. Why couldn't the ghost see his parents?

Answer: They were trans-parents.

139. What ghost is the best dancer?

Answer: The boogie man.

~~~~~~~~~~

140. What is a ghoul's favorite game?

Answer: Hide and Ghost seek.

141. What do you get when you cross Bambi with a ghost?

Answer: Bamboo.

~~~~~~~~

142. What is a werewolf's favorite meeting place?

Answer: A pack meeting.

143. Why don't ghosts like rain?

Answer: It dampens their spirits.

~~~~~~~~~~~~

144. What is a goblin's favorite cheese?

Answer: Monster-ella.

145. Whom do monsters buy their cookies from?

Answer: The ghoul scouts.

〰️

146. What is Dracula's favorite circus act?

Answer: The juggler.

147. What is a vampire's favorite dance?

Answer: The Fang-Dango.

~~~~~~~~

148. Why are vampire's so easy to fool?

Answer: Because they are suckers.

149. What do you call a vampire that lives in the kitchen?

Answer: Count Spatula.

~~~~~~~~~~~~~~~~~~

150. What do you get if you cross a vampire with a teacher?

Answer: Lots of blood tests.

CPSIA information can be obtained
at www.ICGtesting.com
Printed in the USA
LVHW01s0709061117
555122LV00004B/17/P